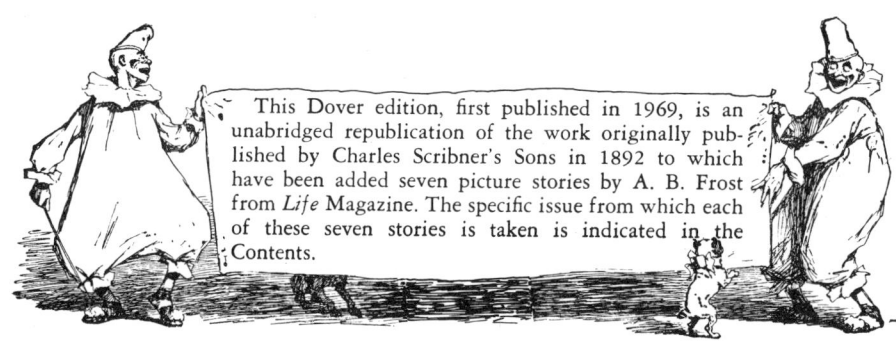

This Dover edition, first published in 1969, is an unabridged republication of the work originally published by Charles Scribner's Sons in 1892 to which have been added seven picture stories by A. B. Frost from *Life* Magazine. The specific issue from which each of these seven stories is taken is indicated in the Contents.

Standard Book Number: 486-22230-6
Library of Congress Catalog Card Number: 69-17099

Manufactured in the United States of America
Dover Publications, Inc.
180 Varick Street
New York, N. Y. 10014

		PAGE
1.	The Humane Man and the Bull Calf	5
2.	A Warning to Mutton that Thinks Itself Lamb	19
3.	Antonio and Jeremiah; an Inharmonious Tale	29

		PAGE
4.	*Dizzy Joe*	*37*
5.	*Violet's Experience*	*55*
6.	*The Entire Discomfiture of Uneasy Walker*	*63*
7.	*'Twas a Poem about Gentle Spring*	*73*
8.	*The Kidnapping of Private Jean François: A Frontier Episode of the Next War*	*87*
9.	*A Low Down Trick; or, Louisa's Capitulation*	*101*
10.	*A Tale of Two Tails*	*108*

SEVEN PICTURE STORIES FROM LIFE MAGAZINE

                                                                                             PAGE

11. *Deacon Smithers Takes a Short Cut Across the Hardguy Golf Links* (MAY 21, 1921)   113

12. *The Tale of the Hasty Hoboes* (JULY 21, 1921)   120

		PAGE
13.	*Mandy's Stocking* (JULY 28, 1921)	122
14.	*He Got Madder and Madder and Madder* (SEPTEMBER 29, 1921)	131
15.	*The Swimming Party* (JANUARY 19, 1922)	138
16.	*The Second-Hand Cello and The Early Morning Lesson* (JULY 13, 1922)	147
17.	*A Walking Tour* (JULY 13, 1922)	151

The Humane Man and the Bull Calf.

"Make veal of that pretty creature! 'T is a shame!" says the Humane Man. "I will buy him and take him home to the children."

"Ef Oi was you, Oi wud niver toi that rope around me waist," says the former proprietor of the calf.
"Oh, never fear; he is a gentle thing," says the Humane Man.

The "gentle thing" develops a tendency to play rather startling to the Humane Man.

And takes him for a little dash down a stony hill,

But is stopped at the bottom by a small dog.

"Be still, little calfy, till I untie this cord—that's a good little calfy," says the Humane Man.

Renewal of hostilities by the dog, and a circus performance by the Humane Man and his purchase.

Sudden termination to the circus performance owing to the want of more rope. "You microcephalous idiot," says the Humane Man, "if I had a knife I'd——"

——but the sentence is never finished, for again the dog interferes and the Humane Man is unfurled.

The "pretty creature" becomes really alarmed and goes through a break in the fence leaving the Humane Man in a serious position.

Rescue of the Humane Man by natives — mutual astonishment.

"Boys," says the Humane Man, "you may have that calf—he is yours on condition that he is made at once into *veal—minced veal!!*"

An adventure that befel Maria and Tobias.
A warning to Mutton that thinks itself Lamb.

"Look at that hill, Maria; when we was children how we did roll down hills like that. Wouldn't it be fun now?"

"Lor'! Toby! we're too old and fat fer the likes of that."

"Fat nothin'! come on, let's do it?"

"Well, you go ahead, I'll foller."

"Hi! Maria, aint this glorious?—like we was children agin!?"
"I don't know, Toby, I think I'll stop!"

"Hold on, Maria; stop me!!!"   "Hold on to what, you ole fool, stop yerself!"

"Them—was—briars—Maria!!"   "Think—I'm—'s—big—fool—as—you?"

"Hol'—on—Maria—hol'—on."   "I—won't—ol'—fool!"

"Are you there, Maria?" "Hol' on tight, Maria, we may start agin any minit!"
"What's left of me's here!" "I wish *you* would, and never stop!"

"Well, you're a nice lookin' objeck, Maria."
"If I look half as bad as you, I want to die right here!"

Voices of the night: "You ole fool, I wish I'd never seen you."
"Fool who? You proposed it, Maria!" etc., etc.

Antonio and Jeremiah, an inharmonious tale.

Mr. Hankins:—"I 'clar it's a shame to burn up a good suit ov cloze like dem, jist when de man's gittin well, too!!"

Mr. Hankins:—"Foh de lan's sake! I haint got a match! and dey aint a house widin a mile ov dis!! Have to go git one though!"

Dizzy Joe, the Wanderer:—"Well, here's luck! The gen'l'min's gone in ter swim and fergot to cum out. Looks as if they'd jist fit me!"

Dizzy Joe: "I hope these cloze won't be as hard ter git out of as they was to git in ter! I'll jist give him my ole uns soze he'll have *somethin'* to wear!"

Mr. Hankins:—"*Jerusalem de golden!* I never see a suit ov cloze go to pieces quick ez dat suit of cloze did; dey must be jist chock full er germs!" (*Dizzy Joe takes in the situation.*)

Voice from behind the fence:—"Lemme out!!! Come back you black sinner and help me out!! Help!! Murder!!"

Dizzy Joe:—"I—didn't—expect—to—have—to—take no bath—this—year but—if—I—must—

". . . .—I must."

Dizzy Joe:—"I don't believe Adam and Eve ever made no suit of cloze outer leaves. I'd like ter ketch that black hyena that burned up my Sunday duds."

(*A month later.*) Mr Peter Hisites:—"This *is* great. The quiet solitude of the mighty woods *and* a good lunch is what fits *me*."

Dizzy Joe:—"Excuse me, sir! I—whatsermatter?"

Dizzy Joe:—"I was only about to remark, sir, when you slipped off the log, that I would like to buy one of them sangwishes if you'll take my note for it at thirty days."

Mr. Peter Hisites (*ten minutes later*):—"Do you catch on? We'll make fifty dollars a week apiece and our board an' washin' out of it!"

Mr. Peter Hisites:—"As I was sayin', there's more'n one way of wearin' a coat."

Mr. Peter Hisites:—"Step up, gen'l'min! Here's the wild man of Hankhunkamunk; captured him myself, after a desperate resistance, jist as I am. He's very dangerous; I carry a gun all the time."

Dizzy Joe (*to his spouse*) :—" My dear, this beats wanderin' on a mountain in a straw ulster, and livin' on jerked black snake and blueberries—you bet!!"

Violet's experience.

"You Lucullus Juniper! Has yo' done gone into yo' secon' chile-hood? What you bringin' ole woreout cast-iron images wif dey arms broke off roun' here fo'?"

"Don' you pester yo'sef 'bout dat figger Emmerline Jane; dat's a little surprise fo' Vi'let!"

"Now you Vi'let, dis here gen'l'min is a mos' pertickler fren' ov mine. If I go 'way an' leave you, I don' want none ov yo' kicken tricks; you heah me?"

"Dat's a mos' pertickler fren' ov his'n; well, I should smile!"—

—"but bizness is bizness, an' here goes—!"

"———!!!!!"

"Brer 'Cullus, yo' 'pears to be mighty cheerful fo' a man dat's standin' on the aidge ov de grave!"
"I ain' gwine ter die jist yit, Brer Hacklefeather!"
"Ain' dat yo kicken' muel Vi'let?"
"Dis here my muel Vi'let, but she ain' a kicken mule no mo'! She done had a 'sperience!"

The entire discomfiture of Uneasy Walker.

Hatching the plot.

Setting the bait.

Waiting for the signal.

The action begins.

Is continued with warmth.

The situation becomes desperate.

Dictating the terms of surrender.

The capitulation.

'Twas a Poem About Gentle Spring.

Editor of the Weekly Whoop (*alone*):—"Been up all night with the baby, head aches, three libel suits on hand, men on strike, subscriptions falling off, what next? Murder would be a pastime fer me now—— Come in!!!"

Editor W. W.:—"*What!* a poem on Spring! I'll spring you——!!!"

"Small Quiet Party:—"Excuse me, sir, jist hold on a minute—

"I didn't expect to have to do no fightin', but if I *must* I'll have to get this 'ere coat off. Jist go up there a half a second!!"

Editor:—" Wha— Wha— What do you want?"

Small Party:—" I was a-givin' Mr. Snees, the poet, a sparrin' lesson an' he says, jist slip my coat on an' run over to the *Weekly Whoop* with this 'ere Spring poem, while I git me breath."

Editor W.W.:—" Who are *you*?"

Small Party:—" Jist excuse me—

a half a second—

and—

I'll give you—

my card——Professor Bolero, Cannon Ball Tosser and Lightning Change Artist, sir, to the Crowned Heads of Europe, sir."

Small Party:—"I'm a poor man, sir, with a large family, sir, an' I'd be very thankful for any small jobs, sir, like givin' you sparrin' lessons, or massage, or takin' care of the furnace, sir!"

Editor W. W.:—"Well, call in again, Professor. This is my busy day."

Editor W. W.:—"*Come in!!*"

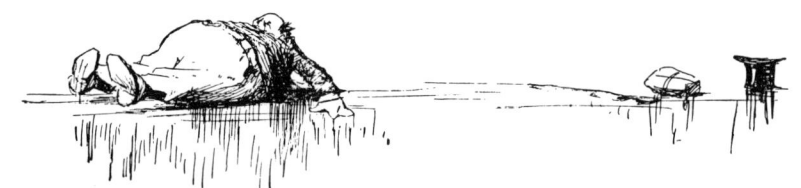

The Kidnapping of Private Jean François: a frontier episode of the next war.

A low down trick or Louisa's capitulation.

"Dat's a bad trick yo' muel Louisa's got, Brer Jackson!"
"I done bruk ebery shubel an' broom on de place on dat muel an' kyant cure her, Brer Peters."
"I kin, Brer Jackson!"
"Brer Peters, ef you cure that muel I gwine giv' yo' two pullets an' a water-million."

"I'se gwine off heah in de bushes, an' ef yo' a honorable muel like w'at you looks like, yo' gwine to stan' still, an' no pullin' on dat ole rope, w'at ain't strong, nohow; you heah me?"

"Look a' dat, Brer Jackson; look a' dat!"
"Ki, Brer Peters, ain' she a-gwine?"

"Is yo' hurt, Louisa? Po' Louisa! I reely 'stonished w'en I see yo' git a fall like dat."
"Did yo' foots slip, Louisa? W'at make yo' jump in de water dat-a-way?"
"Po' Louisa!"

"Louisa look kin' a down-hearted Brer Jackson."

"Dey ain' no mo' pull back in that muel; I jist keep de blinkers on her and tie her wif a piece of cotton thread dese days."

A tale of two tails.

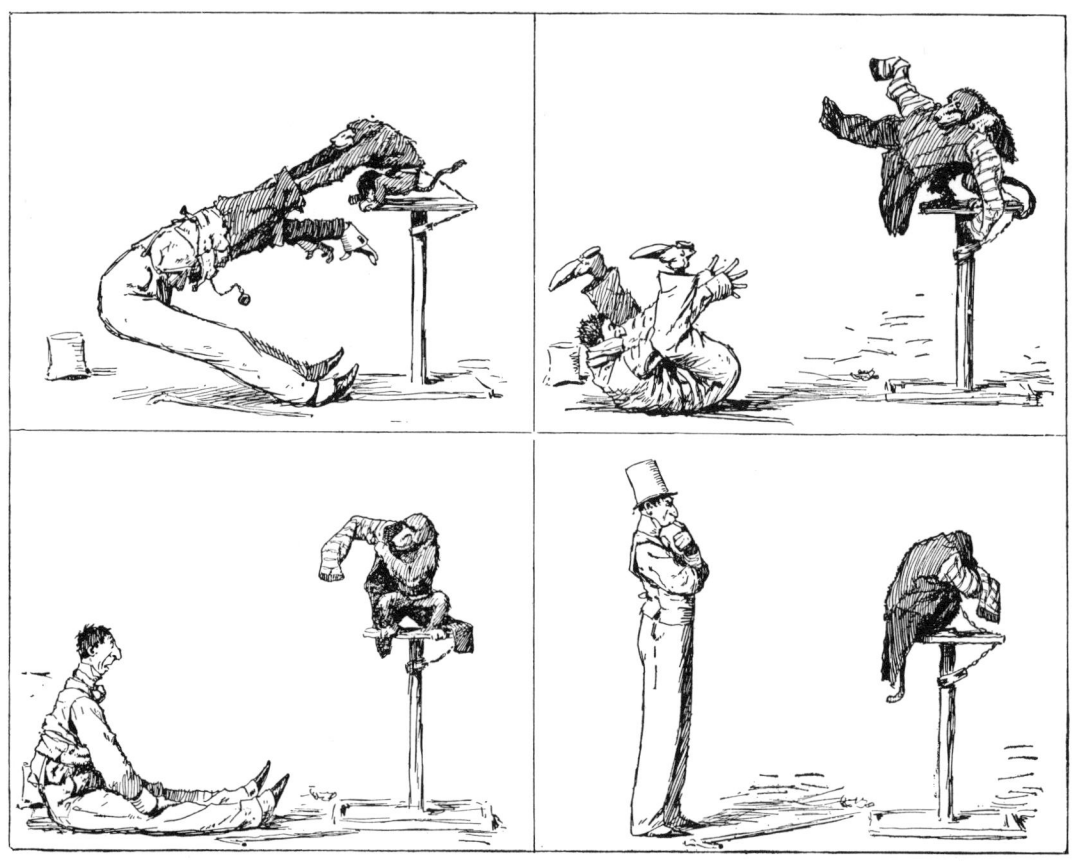

Deacon Smithers Takes a Short Cut Across the Hardguy Golf Links.

The Tale of the Hasty Hoboes

Mandy's Stocking

*He Got Madder
    and Madder and Madder*

He drives a ball into the pond

Drives thirteen balls into the pond

Throws his club into the pond

Throws his bag into the pond

Throws his caddy into the pond

Throws himself into the pond
(N. B.—He played next day as usual)

The Swimming Party

The Farmer: Put your bear in there and come up to the house—I'll give you somethin' to eat.

The Hired Man: I'll put this harness away and then I'll go to dinner. I'm as hungry as——

"a bear!!"

The Farmer: Holy Moses! Look at them cows! Look at them fences! If I catch that Bum I'll kill him!

The Bear: Why did he do that? I only wanted to play with him!

The Tramp: Miserable black villain—I'll knock-a your head off!

The Farmer: Git in thar! I'll learn ye to bring yer cow-killin' bears onto my place.

The Bear: You go in there and I'll be with you in about a minute!

The Second-Hand Cello and The Early Morning Lesson

He thought the clock went off.

She's sure it's a murder.

The veterinary tries an antidote.

This one goes cuckoo altogether.

A Walking Tour